Survival Ha~~ndbook~~
for
Freaked-out Parents

An A-Z guide for when your kids hit their teens

Eleanor Watkins

First published in 2000 by
KEVIN MAYHEW LTD
Buxhall
Stowmarket
Suffolk IP14 3BW

1 2 3 4 5 6 7 8 9

ISBN 1 84003 559 5
Catalogue No. 1500359

Cover design and illustrations by Simon Smith
Edited and typeset by Elisabeth Bates
Printed in Great Britain

Introduction

I had a few doubts when I was asked to write this guide for parents as a follow-on to my *Teenage Girl's Survival Handbook*. My husband and I had raised four children through the teen years and had our share of problems and difficulties, as well as the fun and enjoyment and rewards. With hindsight, we had also made our share of mistakes. It was mainly the knowledge of these mistakes that made me hesitate.

However, I thought again, and decided to go ahead. I believe that we all – parents and children – can learn from our mistakes as well as from the things we did right. I believe that, with God in our lives, even the worst dilemmas and situations can be turned to good. I believe that love can cover a multitude of failings.

If you're a parent struggling with teenage problems, take heart! Be encouraged to know that the chances are you'll win through and be stronger to fight the next battle! Despite some opinions, there are thousands of fine young people coming to maturity in these days, so lots of you must be getting it right! Don't be afraid to seek help if you need it – there is much wise counsel and support available for the asking. Above all, learn to lean hard on God, who is your children's Father and a loving Father to you, too.

Acceptance

See also
**Encouragement,
Self-esteem**

There is a deep need at the heart of every single person, whatever their age, to be accepted for who and what they are. This need is particularly acute during the confused (and confusing) years of adolescence, though a young person may not fully understand what he or she is feeling. The need to belong can often push young persons into conforming to the values and behaviour of a peer group, even if it goes against the teachings they have received. We are social beings, not created to be alone, and we need to belong.

Children need to know from an early age that they were made by God, that God knows them through and through, and loves and fully accepts them just as they are. The best way to demonstrate this is within the context of a loving, stable, secure family background, where every member is fully loved and accepted, warts and all!

Advice

Most parents love to dish out advice, asked for or not. A bit of caution may be in order here. We may think we know best (and we probably do) but a child will learn to turn a deaf ear if it is constantly bashed with stuff they don't want to hear. On the other hand, a timely word can be just what your teenager wanted but didn't like to request. Learn to discern.

Listening to your child may be more valuable than handing out words of wisdom, especially if you only know half a story, or one side of it. And thank God if your child does ask your advice. You are probably the person best qualified to give it.

Alcohol

Alcohol abuse is, sadly, a major problem among young people today, and is the cause of more deaths than the combined total of all other types of drug-related tragedy.

Young people drink because others do, because it initially relaxes them, and because drinking is seen as essential for having a good time. Consumption of alcohol does create a relaxing of inhibitions and a feeling of well-being. It also impairs judgement, damages body organs over time, can become addictive and is a major cause of accident and injury.

Alcoholics Anonymous (AA),
London helpline: 0171 352 3001

Head Office, PO Box 1, Stonebow House, York, YO1 7NJ
(01904) 644026

Alcohol Action Wales,
8th Floor, Brunel House, 2 Fitzlan Road, Cardiff, CF2 1EB

Anger

See also
**Arguments,
Confrontation**

Teenage children can make you angry. They can make you very angry. They can make you hopping mad!

Whatever the reasons – their unreliability, laziness, untidiness, deceit, selfishness or a myriad of others – tempers can flare and harsh and hurtful words be flung about.

Anger may be justified. A showdown is sometimes inevitable. But please, please, try to allow yourself a little time to cool down before initiating that confrontation. Your teenager's defences will come up, and hurtful things may be said and done that can't easily be forgotten. Try never to attack your child verbally in front of their peers and friends. Teenage pride is easily damaged and will make forgiveness harder.

If you feel that in the heat of the moment you acted unfairly, pocket your pride and apologise. You may have an instant response with a hug and make up, or your child may sulk and make you suffer for a bit, but either way you'll be respected for it in the long run.

Anxiety

See also **Worry**

Anxiety can almost be a way of life during your child's teen years. Problems and hazards will grow as your child grows in stature and independence; there will be important decisions to be made and dangerous pitfalls to avoid. We worry about our child's eating and sleeping habits, their friends, their education, their future and all the mistakes they might make.

With God in our lives, we have something far beyond our own resources. We are invited to cast our burdens upon him (Matthew 10). We are told how to cope with anxiety (Philippians 4). If God advises it, it can be done. Thank him and take full advantage of his provision for us.

Apologies

See **Anger**

Arguments

See also **Anger, Confrontation**

There'll be plenty of those with teenagers in the house, especially if you have more than one! Arguments can range from constructive and stimulating discussions, through heated exchanges of opinion, to misunderstandings and downright name-calling, or even physical stuff!

Maybe it's better to let the youngsters sort out their own differences, up to a point anyway. What that point is, you'll have to decide.

Arguments between parent and child can become a habit, with your child automatically disagreeing with any view or opinion you might express. Arguments aren't usually very constructive, and are best avoided. However, don't be browbeaten by your child for the sake of peace. Stand your ground if the issue is something that really affects the child's, or anyone else's, safety, well-being or happiness. The time to back down is when you realise you're keeping the argument going simply to prove that you know better than your child, or if your real motive is concern about what others may think. Don't block out your child's viewpoint, however misguided you know it is. Show them you're concerned enough to really listen instead of just shooting them down in flames.

bB

Bathroom

While your kids are in their teens the bathroom will resemble a disaster area. A teenager has no concept of hanging up wet towels, lifting the lid off a laundry basket to deposit dirty clothing therein or even of drying their feet after a shower so as not to leave a trail of wet splodgy footprints soaking through the carpet. Their jars, cans and bottles of gels, deodorants, sprays, lotions and potions spill out of the cupboards and shelves and crowd out their elders' modest toilet requirements. They (the teenagers) do not clean the bath after using it. They run the hot tap until the tank is empty of water, leaving none for their father's ablutions. Their mother snatches a wash when she can, usually mid-morning or late evening.

There is no advice or comfort to offer parents concerning bathrooms, except that one day your children will leave, and with them will go the wet towels, overflowing laundry bins and smelly socks. Until then, what can't be cured must be endured.

Bible

The Bible has a great deal to say on the subject of parents and children. The book of Proverbs alone is a mine of wise advice. Much of it is good sound practical common sense set against a background of secure family life and values. We can learn about family values from the life of Jesus, too. He grew up in an ordinary home, which at some stage, possibly during his teenage years, became a one-parent family. He demonstrated his growing independence at the age of 12, but afterwards went back and lived in obedience to his elders again. He was certainly one of the breadwinners of his family until his ministry began, but when that time came he had no compunction about leaving his family. His mother did not cling to him, though they must have shared a close bond with each other. Nor did she try to prevent him, but gave him the freedom to do what he had to do.

Blowing your top

See **Anger**

Books

There are many excellent published books on all aspects of parenting to be found in church libraries or Christian bookshops. Books are expensive to buy, but your local library can obtain any title you ask for. Books can be a real help and a rich source of information and encouragement.

I couldn't attempt to begin a list of the excellent books there are available, but I will mention two authors (both female) who have been tremendously inspiring to me personally at times of family crisis. One is Mother Julian of Norwich, with her uplifting *Revelations of Divine Love*. The other is Barbara Johnson of Spatula Ministries, whose wonderful combination of wit, wisdom and reassurance has many times saved my sanity and restored my sense of perspective.

Borrowing

Teenagers don't have a lot of option about borrowing, because they can seldom afford to buy much for themselves. Girls will borrow clothes and make-up from mums and sisters, and return the items crumpled, messed up or used up. Boys of a certain age will attempt to borrow parents' cars, and if successful may return them with an empty tank or a scratch on the paintwork. Money is the trickiest thing to lend to a teenager – you have about a one in a thousand chance of having it returned at all.

Boyfriends

When your daughter brings home a boyfriend for the first time, he may not be quite what you'd been led to believe. She'd probably portrayed him as charming, handsome, mature, and the best thing since sliced bread. The rather awkward, spotty and skinny reality may not quite tie in.

You're not seeing him with her eyes, you may see very little to like in him at all, and you may feel very strongly that he is totally wrong for your daughter.

Whatever you do, don't criticise. Welcome him to your home. If he's really that awful, the scales will drop from your daughter's eyes when she sees him away from the crowd, in the setting of a normal home background.

Then again, your first impressions could be wrong. People often grow on you as you get to know them. You may end up seeing his better points and getting quite fond of him.

cC

Change

It can come as something of a shock to realise that your sweet-natured, well-behaved little son or daughter has turned into a teenager without even asking your permission! Suddenly, your child is thinking, reacting and behaving in ways that seem quite foreign to his or her former nature, and, even worse, foreign to the upbringing and teachings you have instilled!

Change is inevitable. Sometimes it's painful. Your child is growing up (hopefully) into the kind of man or woman God planned, and we don't always understand what happens in the process. A butterfly emerging from its chrysalis needs a degree of safety and protection during the struggle, but also space and freedom to dry and strengthen its wings before flying away.

Remember, too, that all of us are changing, all the time. God has promised that all of his children will be conformed to the image of his Son, and some of the experiences along the way may be painful but necessary. We parents can perhaps serve our children best by allowing God to change us in whatever way he sees fit. He knows the person you will be, and the person your child will be. It may not always be an easy progression, but you'll both get there in the end.

Church

As Christians, we have probably taken our children faithfully to church over the years. Most of us parents remember with mixed feelings those Sunday morning scrambles getting every-one fed, washed, dressed and in their places on time. It was worth it, though, wasn't it, to see 'four little Smiths all in a row, dressed in their Sunday best!'

Things won't stay the same when the kids hit their teens. The scene will change. You are more likely to have one child (in jeans and trainers) sitting with her friends at the back, one playing in the band, one attending a different service altogether, and one out with their friends, having decided that church is a waste of space and not for them.

Don't worry unduly if your child decides they want to worship at another church. Maybe they find the other service more relevant. Maybe there are more young people at the other place – and young Christians need others. Maybe they have questions they are struggling with, and find it easier to find answers with people who haven't known them since they were in nappies. Maybe they're finding it hard to live up to the expectations of your church.

Don't feel you have to make excuses for your child to the church leaders/members. They have a perfect right to go elsewhere if they wish. Don't criticise their choice. Support them in the decisions they make about where to worship. Pray for them, and encourage them to find their own spiritual feet.

Communication

See *also* **Listening**

This is one of the most important things to try to maintain through the ups and downs of the teenage years.

14

Communication with your child may have seemed easy during the childhood years, but can often break down with the onset of adolescence with its hormone activity and mood swings. Your chatty child may become morose and monosyllabic. Their obvious resentment at your questions may cause fears that they have something to hide.

They probably just need their own space and privacy. A prying parent they can do without just now.

On the other hand, let your child know that you are there for them if they do want to talk. Don't fob them off or indicate that you are too busy. They might think twice about asking again. If your child does need to tell you something, try and hear them out without interrupting, moralising or giving advice. They may not need advice anyway, just a sounding board or a sympathetic ear to listen while they get something off their chest. Try to stay calm if you hear something you'd rather not. Hitting the ceiling helps nobody and may only alienate your child. Learn to listen. Above all, never betray a confidence, even if you think it's in the child's own interests.

Confrontation

See also
Arguments, Hitting the ceiling

Can't be avoided sometimes but try and choose your moment. Give yourself time to calm down if possible, whatever the circumstances. Try not to rant and rave, or hurl threats or ultimatums. Don't heap blame on your child's friends or acquaintances who may be involved. Hang on to a sense of perspective.

15

Worse things could have happened, couldn't they? Try and see the funny side, and if there isn't one, hang on to the knowledge that God is ultimately in control and that this, too, will pass.

Cults

Parents often get worried about the strange cults and sects – and they are very real – who prey on vulnerable young people. Sometimes Christian groups or organisations are suspected of being a cult, particularly as there are so many clubs, house fellowships, groups and things like Alpha courses that may not be fully understood. If you are concerned about anything your teenager may be getting into, ask if you can go along and sit in on one of their sessions.

Any group which does not welcome parents, or which encourages young people to cut loose from their families, is deeply suspect.

If your child has already become involved with a cult, there are organisations that can help.

Dads

See also **Fathers**

If you are a dad you can't fail to notice that your role changes as the kids hit their teens. Earlier, your children will have waited eagerly for your return from work, clamoured to go out with you, believed you could fix any problem, and generally looked up to you.

Now, suddenly, you may find you are something of an embarrassment to them. They are critical of your uncool appearance and your interests, and avoid being seen with you in public (except on occasions where transport is needed). They are unwilling to take your advice, consider your views well out of date, and give the impression you're not much use for anything except paying the bills.

What went wrong? Nothing really. They're discovering they have identities of their own, pushing their boundaries, testing their limits. They're growing up.

The teen years can be hard on dads. They'll test your patience, love and understanding to the limits and then some. But you'll come through. The kids will reach maturity and you'll regain your peace, your status, your sanity, your spare time and some of your belongings – plus a set of young people who will hopefully be some of your best friends.

Deception

As parents (especially Christian parents), we'd all like to think that we have an honest and open relationship with our children, that we can trust them to be truthful and that they would come to us with any difficulty.

In an ideal world, this might be the case. But all of us, parents and children, are imperfect people in an imperfect world. Your kids won't tell you everything. (Did you, with your parents?) They may bend the truth a bit now and then. The odd lie or two may come to light. A bit of deception may go on.

Try not to come down too hard on your child if found out in a lie. Truth is important but the teen years are difficult times and characters are still being formed. Discuss the importance of truth as calmly as you can with your child. Convince them that you really do want to trust them. And take a careful look at any areas of hypocrisy there may be in your own lives.

Depression

See also
Hormones, Moods

Hormones are running riot in the teens, causing a whole range of moods and feelings. Mood swings are quite normal for both sexes. Highs can turn to lows and vice versa in a very short space of time.

However, teenagers can become depressed about relationships that aren't working out, or exam pressures, or family situations, or their own feelings about themselves. Keep an eye on someone who becomes withdrawn, or who often breaks down in tears, or who is tired all the time but still can't sleep. There may be nothing seriously wrong, but a checkup with their GP will do no harm. Depression can be very effectively treated, with medication or counselling, or a combination of both.

Diet

See also **Weight**

Both boys and girls develop at a furious rate in their teens, and a healthy diet is vital. Good eating habits start early, so it's not much use trying to promote a healthy eating regime if they've been brought up on convenience foods. Getting them involved in planning and cooking family meals helps them learn nutritional values as well as giving them a start in fending for themselves. Use plenty of fresh foods, including lots of salads, veg and fruit (five pieces of raw fruit or veg a day is a healthy eating habit).

However, it won't hurt them to indulge now and then in the odd McDonald's, Chinese take-away or fish and chips.

Disappointment

Your children will probably disappoint you, in one way or another, sooner or later. All of us parents have hopes, aspirations and dreams for our children which may or may not coincide with their own ideas or capabilities.

Possibly the worst disappointment is to see a child begin to fulfil its potential in the way that seems exactly right for it and then suddenly veer from the pathway on to a quite different (and sometimes disastrous) course.

Don't forget that God's ways are not our ways, his thoughts not our thoughts. He has his own plans for our children, and he knows the end from the beginning. Sometimes we have to stand back and let him work in a child's life, trusting in his love and complete understanding. Take your disappointment to God, rather than giving in to the temptation to heap reproach upon your child.

Discipline

Discipline has to start early. If your child hasn't learned to respond to discipline at 4, they are unlikely to take kindly to it at 14.

Discipline is scriptural (try reading through Proverbs). It's not about punishment, or forcing your own views on your child. It's about love, and security. A child needs to know their boundaries to feel safe and secure. They need to test and push these boundaries as they grow older.

Methods of discipline may vary from family to family, or even from child to child. Leaving a child undisciplined is doing them a great disservice. A child who learns to accept discipline is likely to grow into a self-disciplined adult, who in turn will be able to take responsibility for others.

Divorce

Divorce is hard on children, and perhaps teenage children especially. Sadly, it's also increasingly commonplace, even among Christians. It's difficult to accept, but it's a fact.

Unfortunately, when parents are hurting and agonising over their personal problems, it's all too easy to minimise the suffering of the children. Please don't assume that because teenagers seem to be carrying on as normal and going out with their friends, that they're not hurting too. Teenagers suffer terribly when things go wrong with their families. If you have problems, don't shut them out or put them off with half a story. They'll see through that in a flash. Sit down and talk to them, explain as well as you can what is happening and try to include them in any decisions that have to be made. Don't put too much responsibility on them though – it's too much for even a mature teenager to have to carry the emotional pain of a parent. Don't be tempted to criticise the other parent to your child, however much you may feel they're in the wrong. A child needs to love and respect both parents, whatever their failings.

Above all, don't let the child or children think that it's their fault in any way. Teenagers do put pressure on that may be the last straw in an already struggling marriage, but it's too heavy a load for a young person to have to carry for the rest of his or her life.

Drama

You don't need to visit a theatre to watch a good drama if you have a teenager in the house. Both boys and girls of a certain age and temperament thrive on drama and can wring the last drop from any situation. Anything from a defeat at football to a small spot erupting on an otherwise flawless skin can provoke tears, tantrums and high drama, all for free. It's a bit wearying for the family, but maybe not altogether bad. A dramatic outburst can be a kind of safety valve, a bit like the steam vent on a pressure cooker, helping to prevent a worse explosion.

Drinking
See also **Alcohol**

Alcohol consumption appears to have reached an all-time high among young people. Statistics show that there are more deaths related to excessive intake of alcohol than to all other forms of drug abuse put together.

21

Christian families have to make their own choices about their attitudes to drinking. The Scriptures warn about excess in both the Old and New Testaments, but seem to indicate that a little wine will do no harm and may even be beneficial. A glass of wine with a meal or a pint at your local may be acceptable to you or it may not.

Your own example, whatever it may be, will have an effect on your children, though perhaps not necessarily the one you expect. Children from a secure, happy family are less likely to go over the top in any area, including drinking.

Driving

When your child reaches 17, driving will become an option, especially if you are not in an area with good public transport. If your son or daughter wants to learn to drive, lessons from a qualified instructor are best. A dad (or mum) teaching a child to drive sometimes works, but is more likely to create friction.

During the run-up to 17, you are likely to have spent many hours taxiing your child to and from school, sports, clubs, friends, nights out, etc. When your child passes the driving test, you may welcome the change from being tied to their schedules and think you're seeing the last of phone requests to be picked up at 1.30am.

Sorry, but post L-plates you'll still be missing out on sleep, biting your nails, and wondering if the examiner's judgement was sound and whether your child can *really* be trusted on the road – especially if they've borrowed your car.

Drugs

A great deal has been written about the dangers of drug-taking, and I won't attempt to add much here. An excellent publication entitled *Drugs – what you need to know* can be picked up at any surgery, health centre or youth club, and describes in detail the various drugs, solvents and substances open to abuse, their effects and their dangers.

Alternatively, the National Drugs Helpline offers free and confidential advice (including information about services available in your area) and can be reached 24 hours a day on 0800 776600.

eE

Embarrassment

Teenage children are easily embarrassed, especially by the clothes, hairstyles, household decor, music and opinions of their parents; the way they speak, eat or laugh – it all makes them squirm. However hard you try you won't get it right. Try not to be hurt if your son or daughter asks to be picked up round the corner, or two blocks away from where you live. It's just not good for their street-cred to be seen in public with a parent or, even worse, with both parents.

Emotions

See also **Anxiety, Depression, Hormones, Moods**

Emotions are volatile in the teen years, soaring to the heights and plummeting to the depths and back again in a short space of time. It's the hormones again, and it's all quite normal. Things will level out in time.

Don't underestimate a teenager's capacity for genuine depth of emotion though. Teenagers feel deeply and they're vulnerable. They're capable of experiencing every bit as much pain as an adult when, for example, there's a bereavement, a family break-up or a split with a boy- or girlfriend, but without the experience and maturity to fully understand and cope with what they're going through. A teenager in this situation needs all the support and understanding they can get.

Empty Nest Syndrome

This is something possibly experienced more by mums than dads. Whether or not she has her own career, a mother will have had her children as the central pivot of her life. When the last one leaves for college, uni, work or whatever, the sense of loss can be devastating.

For years you may have yearned for more time to yourself, freedom from school runs and other chauffeuring duties, a tidy house, peace and quiet, and so on. Now it's happened. The last child has left. There's no morning rush for school buses. The hi-fi is silent. The phone bills and the laundry have shrunk. The house is tidy and no longer invaded by noisy, hungry teenage friends. You are free as a bird to come and go as you like. And you feel lost.

It's a tough time, but a transitional one. You will adjust. Gradually, the house will begin to feel peaceful rather than just empty. You'll start to enjoy it. The two of you will discover the pleasures of being a couple again, rather than a family. You can take a course in gourmet cookery, or line dancing, or computer literacy. You could join a women's group or prayer circle, or your church may be glad of your help in all kinds of ways. If you miss the company of young people, there are young couples or single mums who might welcome your friendship.

Try to face these changes in a positive way and make the most of them. It won't be long until the term ends and they're all home for the holidays!

Encouragement

A little bit of encouragement is worth a whole load of criticism. Teens, like everyone else, need to feel good about themselves and to know that they're OK people. They may not always show they appreciate it, and it may not always be easy to do, but a little bit of praise from a parent will go a long way towards building confidence and positive attitudes.

Example

Your example will speak volumes, much more than anything you can say. Today's teenagers won't stand for hypocrisy, and even younger children can spot the hollowness of a 'do as I say, not as I do' attitude.

Exams

Exam times are hard on everyone. A sensible and balanced outlook is needed in the run-up to GCSEs, A-levels or any other exams. Your child needs your support in the form of quietness and space to study, regular meals, help when they ask for it and encouragement to do the best they can (though not to the point of pressure that makes them feel that passing this exam is the only thing that matters – it isn't). Failed exams can always be re-sat, and there are always other routes to their goal.

Try and see that your child gets some relaxation, sees friends, takes exercise – even in the midst of the most intense revision. There's life after exams, whatever their results, so try and keep a sense of perspective. Perhaps most important of all, be there for your child when they need to talk, and uphold them in prayer.

Failures

See also **Faults**

Everyone fails from time to time. None of us breezes through life making a success of everything we undertake, and it's good that we don't. We learn from our failures, not only to do better but also to walk humbly and to be able and willing to accept help, advice and guidance from fellow humans and from God.

If your child fails – in their own expectations or in yours or those of others – don't let them feel it's the end of the world. It isn't. Help them to learn positive lessons from the experience, to cope with disappointment and to try again, maybe in a different direction . . .

Families

See also **Dads, Fathers, Mums, Grandparents**

The family structure nowadays is not always simply mum, dad and kids. With soaring divorce rates (among Christians too) a family will often contain a step-parent and/or stepchildren and maybe half-brothers or sisters. This makes life more difficult and complicated for the children and extremely hard work for parents. Assorted mixtures of adults and children do not automatically gel together to make one big happy family. But with dedication and a sense of humour, patience and above all, prayer, a step-family can work, and step-siblings can become good friends and allies.

Fashion

Fashions come and go. They did in our day and they do now. Teenagers these days mostly seem to live in sportswear and trainers, and we might wish they'd dress up now and then and do themselves justice. Or is it just to satisfy our own pride?

Don't let's kid ourselves, though, that we get away cheaply with such casual wear. Those designer-label price tags are something to faint from.

Fathers
See also **Dads**

Being a father is an awesome responsibility. A father is head of his family, usually the provider (or main provider), protector, defender, encourager and role-model to his children. The kind of father you are will be, at least in part, determined by the kind of fathering you received yourself. If you were valued, loved and affirmed by your father, you will be well equipped to do the same for your own sons and daughters.

But, even if your own father failed in certain areas, it doesn't have to mean that you will necessarily follow suit. When God is given control of your life, he can more than make up for any parenting qualities you may lack. Don't forget, God is a Father to your children, and he is your Father too.

Faults
See also **Failures**

We are faulty beings and we live in a faulty world. As in certain geographical locations (i.e. the San Andreas Fault in California), we have areas of weakness that, given certain conditions, can blow up into real trouble.

Trying to convince our teenagers that we are perfect individuals who never make mistakes is not clever. For one thing, they won't be fooled. Teenagers (and younger kids) can see as far through a brick wall as anyone. Much better to be open about our weaknesses.

If we're honest about our faults, we're more likely to be able to help our children avoid the same or similar ones. Don't be afraid to apologise when you've misjudged or overreacted to something your child has said or done. They'll respect you for it in the long run.

Forgiveness

Forgiveness lies deep at the root of every successful relationship because it is the basis of our relationship with God. In Christ, we are forgiven, accepted and loved.

Each child, no matter what mistakes they have made, or how badly they have messed up, needs to know that same forgiveness, from God and from their family. An unforgiving spirit will hurt the one who has transgressed, but it will hurt the one refusing to forgive even more, and it is poison to relationships.

If you feel you can't forgive your child, ask God to soften your heart. He can do it and he will.

Freedom

Giving an adolescent child the gradual freedom to take control of their own life, to take decisions, even to make their own mistakes and hopefully to learn from them, is a necessary part of parenting. It's not always easy. Our instincts are to protect and shield our children from the perils of the world, from harmful influences and sometimes from their own rebellion and the disastrous pathways they seem intent on taking.

We can see pitfalls that they can't, and dangers that they laugh at. Letting out the reins is a tricky operation, but it must be done, and is best done gradually, with prayer and care.

Friends

You may like some of the friends your teenagers bring home, but there may be some you don't take to at all.

Try not to criticise or run them down to your child – it will only have the effect of making them stick closer. Try to see what it is your child likes about a particular friend. See them as a person in their own right, with feelings and opinions, and not just as someone who will influence your child. But be discreet – your main function is to be a parent rather than a pal.

Future

Not a great many teenagers have detailed plans for their own futures. There may be some dedicated young people who have their lives mapped out in their minds, but these will be the minority. Most are trying to make sense of life, find their own identity and purpose, discover what they believe or don't believe, and have some fun while they sort it all out.

Remember that God does have a plan for your child's life, but it may not be the same as your plans for him or her. Encourage your children to seek God for themselves, and try to accept and support them whatever they decide, even if it's giving up their studies and going off to work in the Third World. Pray for them and trust God to guide them for their future.

gG

Girlfriends

See also **Jealousy**

The day will come when your son brings his first girlfriend home to meet you. This event will evoke mixed feelings, especially if you are his mother. You will have been the most important female in your son's life so far, and may now have to accept that he has eyes for no one but this reed-slim (usually), trendy, fascinating (to him, anyway) teenage creature.

Be wise. Despite her air of confidence, it's much more of an ordeal for her than it is for you. Don't be surprised if she seems on the clingy side towards your son. It's more to do with boosting her security than staking a claim. Don't be too pushy, but be sure that she's included in the conversation. Don't make too many family in-jokes, and try not to talk too much about people and situations she doesn't know. Maybe a quick coffee is better at the first meeting than a full-scale family meal.

Try and make your son's girlfriend feel welcome in your home. Whether or not the relationship lasts, he'll thank you for it.

God
(as a parent)

It may not come easily to some to think of God first and foremost as a parent, but that is what he is, above all else. God is the loving, compassionate Father who brought us into being and who understands and cares about every detail of our lives. He's the parent who

34

accepts us just as we are, who loves us just the same whether we succeed or fail, and who never gives up on us.

If our children grow up knowing this, we have given them the best possible start in life.

Grandparents

Grandparents are a precious gift, both to a child and to its parents, and fortunate is the child who has a complete set. A teenager often finds it easier to confide in a grandparent than mum or dad – grandparents are less likely to expect too much or to be too disappointed when 'failures' happen. A grandparent is long-sighted, viewing situations from a distance which takes some of the stress out of con-frontation. This long view also gives clearer perspective. A grandparent has been a parent too, has made mistakes and learned from them, and can be a veritable gold mine of wisdom and encouragement to children and grandchildren.

Guilt

Guilt is not a popular concept in today's world.

We are programmed to believe that we have a right to pursue and possess whatever we think will make us happy, sometimes at the expense of others.

However, it's not constructive (or scriptural) to load a child with guilt, forcing him to hide or disguise feelings, behaviour or attitudes which may not tie in with what he has learned at home or church. Teaching a child that he will be punished by an all-seeing God for wrong behaviour is destructive, negative, and not at all what Jesus taught.

But, a sense of accountability, the knowledge that certain results will follow certain courses of action, and that responsibility must be taken for oneself, is something that every young person ought to learn.

Hazards

Any caring parent will be aware that life is full of hazards for today's child. As part of a suffering world, Christian parents are not immune from the dangers that beset our families. There is no other answer when Christians question a God of love for allowing the heartaches and heartbreaks that, alas, happen in the most committed of Christian families.

However, we have a glorious promise. God works all things together for good to those who love him and have answered the call to follow him, and he can turn even the seeming disasters into blessings.

The best protection we can give our children against the hazards of this fallen world are our constant prayers.

Helping

Teenage children are not the most helpful of God's creatures. They can turn a blind eye to the most obvious of family needs, and resent being pointedly asked.

However, a parent may occasionally be pleasantly surprised at how helpful and supportive a teenage child can be, often when least expected. Don't bank on it, though. Just count it as a bonus when it happens, and show lots of appreciation.

Hitting the ceiling

See also
Arguments,
Confrontation

This will happen sooner or later, when you discover something you definitely didn't want to hear, like the appalling grades your child has notched up this term; or the damage they have done to your car, borrowed clothing, furniture, reputation or some other prized possession. You may be fully justified, e.g. if your child has caused damage or danger to themselves or others.

Try, though, to play it as cool as possible. Your child will probably be far more upset than you are. They will have a real sense of having let you down.

Don't let things be said in the heat of the moment that will afterwards be regretted. Your relationship with your child is of paramount importance. Wrongdoing will need to be addressed, but try to do it in as positive a way as possible, and with as few recriminations as you can. And don't let your child feel you will never trust him or her again.

HIV

Comprehensive literature on HIV and AIDS can be obtained from your local surgery, health centre or hospital. Information, advice and counselling are available on the following lines:

National AIDS helpline: 0800 567123

The Red Admiral Project: 51a Philibeach Gardens, London, SW5 9ED
0171 835 1495

They provide free specialist counselling for anyone affected by HIV/AIDS.

Holding on

See also **Letting go**

There will be times when holding on is all that you can do. Your child may have rejected your values, rebelled against your rules, and set out on a pathway that you feel can only lead to disaster. You may have done all that you can, and then some, prayed until you can pray no more, and feel that you've reached the end of your tether.

Holding on is all that you can do, but it's also the best that you can do. Hold on in love for your child, whatever they may have done. Hold on to a God who is perfectly in control of every situation and perfectly able to act when the time is right. Hold on to the fact that even when our faith fails, he remains faithful. And hold on to the certainty that, in the darkest of dark hours, God is holding you.

Holidays

See also
Houseparty

However carefully planned, holidays don't make for harmony when you're sharing them with teenage children. You may think you've opted for something that will please everyone, but teenage offspring have a habit of refusing to be pleased.

In general, teens don't enjoy spending holidays with their parents. Whatever is planned, they are quite capable of complaining, sulking, whinging, and making sure that no one else enjoys it either. It's often a relief all round to settle for separate holidays at this stage.

If you and your teenagers must holiday together, a good compromise is to take along, or meet up with, someone their own age. Christian holidays, houseparties and summer projects are some of the most enriching, exciting and rewarding things your child can do. This kind of holiday experience will help them grow and stretch in every way, and they'll have loads of fun too.

Holy Spirit

A parent needs the fullness of the Holy Spirit (as does every Christian). Everyone who has come to faith in Christ is indwelt by his Holy Spirit, but there is more – a filling or baptising in the Holy Spirit which needs to be renewed again and again. Our bodies are the temple of the Holy Spirit, but unfortunately we tend to be 'leaky' and have to ask for frequent refilling.

God's Holy Spirit is given to be our helper, our comfort in time of trouble, the one who grants wisdom when we are in need of it, the one who brings peace and joy even in the midst of life's heartaches. The Holy Spirit is simply the Spirit of Jesus, living in our bodies and enabling us to do the things that Jesus did, and to see and react to people the way God sees and reacts. The Holy Spirit is a priceless gift to parents who are seeking to bring up their children in the right way.

Homesickness

Your child will almost certainly be homesick the first time he or she spends time away from home, even if it's just a couple of weeks on a school trip or exchange visit. We've all shared the anguish of those sad little letters or tearful phone calls, and choked back our own tears as we urge our offspring to stick it out just a little longer.

Homesickness seems to be largely inevitable but short-lived. Your child will find its feet, get involved and make friends and be having a great time even before you've tearfully retrieved the last sock from under that unoccupied bed.

Homework

In an ideal world, your children would get down to homework immediately after the evening meal, stick at it until it's finished, and then have some time to themselves. They may, however, think it's perfectly all right to leave it to the last moment, study during a meal in front of the TV, or with loud music blaring.

Good habits begin early, and it will help if your offspring have a quiet, warm, private place to get their homework done, from primary school days onward. Hopefully this will carry over into the teen years and they'll be happy to study without the distraction of loud music in the background.

Homosexuality

God created us male and female, and heterosexual relationships are his plan for humanity. However, many young people may go through a time of confusion as they grow and develop. A good role model of the same sex is the best encouragement for a young person discovering and accepting their sexuality in today's difficult and changing world.

However, we must not condemn young

41

Homework

homosexuals, but rather extend to them the love of God in our own attitude – maybe this was the lifeline they had been seeking all along.

Any Christian parent faced with a child who tells them that he or she is homosexual will be shocked and devastated. But try at least to keep open the lines of communication – he or she is still your child, and God can work miracles even in this if we will turn to him and lay the whole burden on him.

Honesty

See **Deception**

Hormones

See also
**Depression,
Emotions, Moods**

Rioting hormones are responsible for a great deal of teenage mood swings. Your child may be hyperactive and lethargic in quick succession, aggressive or passive, gregarious or withdrawn, a creature of extremes as the hormones settle into a stable pattern. It can make for friction.

Bear in mind, too, that some mothers of teens may be experiencing the other end of the hormonal cycle, with the onset of menopause. A mum, too, may have her ups and downs which doesn't make living with a teenager any easier. Mothers and daughters may be particularly prone to friction areas just now. On the other hand, the two of them may be surprised to find they have strong allies in one another – sometimes, at least.

Houseparty

See also **Holidays, Youth groups**

If your child asks to go on a Christian house-party – rejoice! and then fork out if you have to – it'll be a brilliant experience. These gatherings are almost always spiritual milestones in the life of a young person, high spots in relationship with and understanding of God and of other people. Friendships forged in these weeks can last a lifetime and yield enormous strengths; faith will deepen, visions expand, and opportunities of all kinds open up.

Housework

See also **Helping**

Any housework voluntarily undertaken by a teenager is a rare phenomenon and should be welcomed as an unexpected bonus.

Humour (sense of)

A must for the parents of teenage children. Many a tense situation can be diffused by seeing the funny side. Parents and children who can laugh together are likely to be able to surmount most difficulties. Teenagers can be very entertaining and very funny, though their humour might not always match yours.

A good laugh is good medicine for all ages.

il

Idealism

Things always seem more black and white when you are young than when the years have rolled by. Young people tend to be idealistic, and this is not a bad way to be. All of us need ideals to aspire to and strive for, to give us purpose.

Sooner or later your child will probably realise that some ideals are impossible to attain; by then, hopefully, he or she will be mature enough to understand that it's not always a sign of failure to settle for something less.

Illness

A good balanced diet, exercise, adequate sleep and emotional security are the best safeguards for your child's health. However, there are times when a young person may be more susceptible to illness. The first year at college or university can be tricky: living in close proximity to others who carry different bugs from different places, the sharing of eating and cooking utensils, and perhaps even indifferent hygiene can all help the spread of illnesses like glandular fever and other viral infections. Try to instil good basic habits into your child while he or she is still at home, for example good personal and kitchen hygiene and healthy eating habits with lots of fresh fruit and vegetables. These simple measures can go a long way to warding off illness.

Inadequacy

All of us parents have times when we feel inadequate. It starts maybe when we come home from the hospital with that tiny scrap of humanity who depends on us for everything. Certainly there will be many feelings of inadequacy when our children hit their teens.

We *are* inadequate. None of us has the parenting lark sewn up or sussed out. All of us need someone beyond ourselves to lean on from time to time.

Families can be a huge support to struggling parents. Grandparents are a gift. Teachers, tutors, pastors, youth workers, advisers of every kind – a vast army of qualified people is also there to call upon in times of need.

Most of all, God is there to lean upon – and he loves us to lean upon him. His father heart fully understands our trials and perplexities. His Holy Spirit is available to us as Christians with resources of wisdom, strength, encouragement, comfort, hope and patience. He can supply everything that we, as humans, lack. No Christian parent need feel inadequate.

Independence

See also **Empty Nest Syndrome**

Almost from their birth we begin to train our children to be able, eventually, to live as independent beings. We help them to walk, talk, feed themselves, learn, achieve, attain – all milestones on the road to independence.

However, it can come as a shock when one day we realise that they really can survive without our care and attention. We can begin to feel a little redundant and pointless at this juncture. However, if your child has just gone off snowboarding in New Zealand or working with street children in Eastern Europe, take heart. You've brought up an independent human being and you've done your job well.

Individual

Your child is an individual, created by God in his own image, but with a unique set of looks, gifts, talents and capabilities. He or she will have inherited things from both parents and from the generations before, but they will not be exactly like any of you. They won't tread the same pathway you trod, because God has a special plan and purpose just for them.

Insecurity

See also
Self-esteem

Some children have a sense of insecurity which can carry over into teenage and adult life, affecting their attitudes, behaviour and relationships. Adopted children in particular can feel insecure. However loving the family they've grown up in, the adopted child carries the knowledge that, for whatever reason,they were once given away.

A child needs to experience security through unconditional love. He or she needs to be able to know and accept that whatever they're like they're OK – they gain security from their family, their friends and relatives, and most of all by being encouraged to enter into and develop their own personal relationship with God through Jesus Christ.

jJ

Jealousy

See also
**Boyfriends,
Girlfriends,
Sibling rivalry**

The type of jealousy I have in mind may come as something of a shock when it actually hits you. I'm thinking of the feelings experienced when your son or daughter brings home a girl/boyfriend for the first time, and more so as the relationship deepens. This may be especially poignant for a mother and son, or a father and daughter, but may also be keenly felt by the parent of a same-sex child.

Suddenly, you are no longer the pivot of your child's life, no longer the one he or she goes to to talk over problems or share special joys.

A few jealous pangs are probably quite harmless. But be glad that your child is developing normally, and that you've helped him or her in the process.

Get to know the boy/girlfriend and appreciate their positive traits. Above all, whatever your feelings, don't utter a word of criticism about them to your child.

Jesus

Our relationship with Jesus Christ must be at the centre of our faith and worship. There are many doctrines in today's world, a lot of which acknowledge God in some way or other. Your child may come across teachings that suggest that God may be reached by a number of diverse paths, none better or worse than another.

Beware any teaching that denies Jesus as the

49

only way to God (read the Gospel of John). Jesus, though he became fully human during his time on earth, is also fully equal with God, was there with God the Father when the world was created, and will reign with God throughout eternity. Through his suffering and sacrificial death on the cross, Jesus paid the price for the redemption of all who will believe in him. In him, all things are made new. In him, all things are possible. He is our redeemer, saviour, Messiah, healer, husband, brother, friend and coming King.

The greatest Christian witness we can show our children is our own real, living, growing relationships with the Lord Jesus Christ himself.

Killjoys

You may be considered (or called) a killjoy if you dare to restrict your teenager or prevent him or her from doing 'what everyone else is doing'.

Try (if you can) to sit down with your child and talk through the reasons for your restrictions. They may not respond as you'd like, but some of what you say may be absorbed or at least recollected at a later date. Try to listen to their viewpoint and be flexible where you safely can, but don't be bullied by them into agreeing to their wishes just to keep on good terms with them.

There are worse things than being a killjoy.

Late nights

A major bone of contention with teens and their parents. You're likely to hear a lot about those mysterious folk, 'other people's parents', who implicitly trust their children to have common sense and maturity, and so let them keep whatever hours they choose.

Stick to your guns, within limits. It's fine to insist on a time when your young teenager should be home, but listen to their reasons if they request an extension. Check out the circumstances if you have to, but as discreetly as possible – they hate to think you're going behind their back.

Try not to react too strongly when a teenager is home later than they said they would be. You'll be tearing out your hair, but try and listen to the explanation – there may be a good reason. They should have phoned, but it's not always possible. And teenagers are notorious for not seeing the point of view of their elders. Don't let it become a habit though. You need to know they're safe and getting enough sleep.

Laundry

Teenagers create laundry – lots of it. They change often, drop discarded clothing wherever it falls, and expect it to be picked up, washed, dried, ironed and hung up, in pristine condition, ready for the next time they need it. They do not appear to understand how this process happens.

Training your children to do their own laundry is wellnigh impossible. It's hard enough trying to get them to deposit the garments in an appropriate receptacle, instead of under the bed, on the bathroom floor, trailed throughout the house or slung up on top of the wardrobe. The only real relief you'll get from laundry-fatigue is when a child leaves for camp, college or uni.

Even then, it's short-lived. Don't imagine your child is rinsing out socks in a basin, or taking a bag of washing to the launderette. No, they're saving every last piece and will bring it, well-fermented, in bulging black bags on their first visit home. I even know of someone who sent his laundry home by post, inexpertly wrapped and leaking odd socks, shorts and underwear as it travelled.

Leaving

See also **Empty Nest Syndrome, Letting go**

The day will come when your child leaves home. It's inevitable, it's right, and it's what you've been preparing them for for many years.

It's also heartbreaking. Dads may joke about the lovely peace and quiet, and getting their car and telephone back. Mums will feel a devastating sense of loss, and tend to burst into tears in the supermarket when asked about their child.

But, when the goodbyes are being said, she will smile, put on a cheerful face, speak enthusiastically about her child's plans, and send them off feeling positive and looking forward to their new life.

Letters

When there are difficulties between teenage children and their parents and communication has broken down, it can be a frustrating and difficult time for all parties.

Misunderstandings can arise, tempers flare, and words fly in the heat of the moment that can inflict real pain. Fathers and teenage sons can have problems here, and so can mothers and daughters.

A system of communication by letter can be a good safety valve at these times. It's possible to put down on paper what you can't say in words, and also easier to explain the reasons behind our attitudes and actions. The very act of sitting down to collect one's thoughts and set them down on paper is calming in itself, and a letter can be read and pondered on when things are quieter. Try it next time there's trouble. Don't forget to add your love. You may get a reply that surprises and pleases you.

Letting go

See also **Holding on, Leaving**

There is a time to hold on and a time to let go, and sometimes it's hard to tell the difference. Your instinct will be to hold on, help, advise, bail out, give to and support your child. This is good, and it's what being a parent is about.

But a time may come when, whether because of your child's age, or because of the choices they have made, there will be nothing more that you can do or say. This is the time to let go, and allow God to be the one to work in your child's life.

Listening

Listening (really listening) is a real gift that few people really master. It's a great advantage to be able to listen when you have teenagers. Not that they're likely to seek you out and ask you to sit down for a heart to heart, but there will be times when they need to speak and you need to listen. You'd be wise to resist the temptation to interrupt, ask questions, give advice or do anything but hear what your child is saying, paying heed not only to their actual words, but also to what is being said between the lines and what is not being said at all. You'll gain your child's respect for being prepared to take time to listen, and he or she will be more ready to come to you next time a listening ear is needed.

Loneliness

Most teenagers are gregarious beings, but there can be real loneliness too. Christian teenagers in particular can feel out on a limb, especially if they are the only ones refusing to go with the crowd. Loneliness can be a real pressure. It takes a strong personality to stand alone.

Teenagers in rural areas can be especially lonely and isolated. Well-meaning efforts by their elders to get them together with others can sometimes backfire. Teens like to feel they're choosing their own friends.

Christian groups and houseparties are an excellent way of making meaningful and lasting friendships, away from parental guidance. Though friends made this way can be many miles apart, keeping in touch can be a real means of strength and support. Welcome your teenager's friends into your home, to visit or to stay. They won't mind kipping on the floor if they have to.

They'll eat you out of house and home, fill the house with noise and come and go regardless, but they'll have lots of fun, and so will you.

mM

Marriage

Marriage is optional in this day and age. The alternative for young couples is to live together, sharing finance, work and child care as the need arises. It's often cheaper, more convenient and less restrictive. A bit of paper doesn't make that much difference – does it? Or so our young people are led to believe.

It's difficult to explain why to us as Christians marriage is so important. Today's young people have a right to be sceptical when they see the huge percentage of marriage break-ups, even among Christians. That said, despite failures, marriage is still the best option for couples wishing to share their lives. God set a very high value on Christian marriage, likening it to the mystical union between Christ and his bride, the body of believers. Young people growing up with parents who have committed them-selves to each other for life will have no illusions about what marriage is all about. They will have seen the difficulties and the differences, the clash of personalities, the effects of pressure and the problems that arise.

They will also have seen the positive side, the support, the laughter, the fun, the working out of problems and riding out of storms, and the sheer comfort and security of knowing there is always another person there for you.

Giving their child the background of a long-standing committed marriage is the best argu-ment parents can put forward.

Maturity

Sometimes we think our kids are never going to get there. We worry and we agonise as we watch their struggles to grow up and become adults, often making mistakes as they go. We try to help them from our own experience, but this kind of second-hand wisdom rarely works (though they may listen more than we give them credit for). We can be there to help and support, but they need to do their own growing up.

Don't be too anxious. They will make it to maturity, though some may take longer than others. And remember that, as parents, we are still growing and maturing too.

Media pressure

Media plays a huge part in modern living and its pressures are tremendous. You can monitor a young child's TV and video viewing, music and computer games, but not a teenager's. Forbidden things can be watched and experienced at a friend's house or other places.

Try to understand the pressures on your child and discuss with him or her the ideas, images and messages that come across. The more involved your child is with Christian friends, projects, groups and activities, the less likely he or she is to be adversely affected by media pressure. Think about how much you yourself are affected in this way, and make adjustments if you need to. Pray for the protection of your child's mind and will as well as their body.

Menopause

Some mums will be reaching the years of menopause as their teenage daughters hit puberty and adolescence. This is not easy for either party, and a little extra understanding is needed. Your daughter may be difficult, but maybe you're a bit moody too. Rather than antagonise each other, try to offer mutual support. (Not always easy, I know.) Your daughter may have irregular or painful periods before settling into a stable pattern. A menopausal mum may also have tiresome irregularities or heavy bleeding as well as woes such as hot flushes, dry skin or emotional ups and downs. Some women sail through without much trouble, others suffer to some degree. If your life, or your daughter's, is being affected, see your GP or women's clinic. There is plenty of help available for you both.

Mission projects

Christian mission projects, summer camps, volunteer work and the like in this country and abroad are some of the best ways of developing spiritual growth, self-esteem, responsibility and a sense of purpose in young people; added to that are the excitements of travel, learning new skills, making new friends and generally having fun. It'll be worth every penny even if you have to fork out yourself, or your child may begin by raising the money to pay for their place. Below are just a few addresses – there are lots more:

Scripture Union (01908) 856000

Crusaders (Crusoe) 2, Romeland Hill, St Albans, Hertfordshire

World Horizons, North Dock Centre, Llanelli, Dyfed

Mistakes

All of us make them. Mostly we live to regret them, but often we learn and benefit from them too.

As parents, we'll try our hardest to protect our children from making mistakes, especially the ones we made ourselves. They might take notice, but it's more likely they'll have to learn from their own experiences.

A Christian (parent or child) has one great advantage though. God doesn't want us to make mistakes, but if we do, he is in the business of not only understanding and forgiving, but also of turning around even our worst mistakes and bringing good out of them.

Money

Generally speaking, a teenager and their money are soon parted. Most parents wonder where on earth it goes, and find this an expensive time in their child's life. Try not to make too much of an issue about money. If your child has an allowance, make it realistic. A bit of discussion and review may be necessary from time to time.

It's not unreasonable to expect your teenage child to give some help with household chores in exchange for their allowance. Alternatively they could earn some money for themselves with a Saturday or holiday job.

Moods

See also
**Hormones,
Maturity,
Menopause**

Moods are inevitable in teens and are mostly down to hormone activity. They'll even out in time. Try not to react too strongly, however horrid the mood or unreasonable the moody one. They'll probably be back to their own sweet self tomorrow.

Mums

A mum is the cornerstone of a teenager's life. Dads are important too, but it's you, their mum they'll head for when they want sympathy, food, clean clothes, a listening ear and someone to fight their corner; when they want a lend of your car, or your silk shirt, or your new CD, or your shampoo, or a few bob to tide them over.

Music

No teen can live without music. They need it to help them study, to relax, to socialise, to be alone with, to worship, to party, to express themselves, communicate, calm down, cheer up, or to console them when awful things happen.

A teen without music is like lemonade without the fizz.

nN

No

'No' can be a controversial word to use when dealing with teenagers. The child who's never learned to take no for an answer at 3 or 4 is not going to accept it at 13 or 14. Even in well-disciplined families, it's better to sit down and examine the options rather than deliver a straight veto.

There are times, though, when a plain 'no' has to be the only answer if, for instance, what your child is requesting is illegal or dangerous to themselves or others.

It may even come as a relief to a child to realise there's no more room for manoeuvre. Remember, though, that eventually you won't be able to force them to obey, and that they'll know this too. A lot of resentment can build up, which may result in the very situation you're trying to avoid. A good relationship between you will go a long way to negotiating this tricky area.

Noise level

Wherever there are teenagers, there will be noise. Whether it's spectator sport, TV, music, cars and motorbikes, or even worship, they like it loud. You'll be considered old and sad if you ask for anything to be toned down.

You may worry about eardrum damage (probably with cause) but there's not a lot you can do. Unless of course, they're causing real

63

annoyance or distress to others, e.g. elderly people or mums trying to get babies to sleep. Then a little straight talking might be in order. To be fair, they probably never even realised they were being a nuisance.

No

oO

Occult

Young people are curious. They like finding out and trying new things. This curiosity may reach into the supernatural, as many thoughtful young people will wonder about the mysteries of life and what lies beyond.

The word 'occult' simply means 'hidden'. Jesus came into the world to bring light and life, and we are commanded by God to have nothing to do with the 'hidden works of darkness'.

Our children need protection from involvement or even dabbling in things that they may think are harmless – Ouija boards, tarot cards, fortune telling and the like. These things can pave the way for spiritual darkness in the life of a young person. Satan is out to destroy young lives and will make full use of the mysterious and alluring to gain his ends.

The only spirit we need in our lives is the Holy Spirit, the Spirit of Jesus who is goodness and truth. Continuous filling with the Holy Spirit will protect against the lies, deceits and snares of the evil one.

pP

Patience

Your patience will be tried to the limits at times. Teens themselves are not renowned for being patient either. They want things to happen fast, like now, or preferably yesterday.

Waiting is a good discipline for anyone. Teenagers will have to learn to wait for exam results, or to earn enough money for trips or travel, or to work through some course of study and get the required qualifications. Let them see that you too often have to wait, and that the waiting makes it all more worthwhile in the end.

Perhaps the biggest test of your patience will be waiting for them to grow up.

Peer pressure

Never underestimate the power of peer pressure. Teenagers will probably be more influenced by their own age group than they are by parents.

Basically we all need to belong. Teenagers are especially vulnerable, struggling as they are to find their own identity. It's all too easy to conform, even against your better judgement or your own convictions, in order to be accepted and included.

Being part of a group of young Christians is the best safeguard against the wrong kinds of peer pressure. There's strength in numbers. If one is in danger, the others are there to offer caution, help, support and encouragement.

Peer Pressure

Phone

This is another of those major bones of contention, especially when the bills come in. Those long gossipy conversations don't come cheap. Especially infuriating are those sneaky ones made when they thought you were safely out of the way.

You can try restricting your child's phone calls to certain times of the day. You can try enforcing time limits on calls. You can try insisting they pay a certain proportion of the cost of their calls. Anything is worth a go but there's no guarantee it will work for long. You'll get your phone back when they leave home, but then you'll probably get reverse charge calls. You can't win really.

Prayer

Prayer is a mystery, and even the wisest theologians and Bible scholars would admit that they don't understand the half of it. We know that God is omnipotent and omnipresent, the creator of all things who is aware of all circumstances and all needs. Our prayers are not necessary to his plans. Yet, he has chosen to allow us to participate in this way, and what's more, he rejoices and responds when we choose to do so.

The effects of prayer are unlimited. Like a stone thrown into a pond, the ripples go out in all directions. When we pray, for ourselves or others, God's power is released to work in the situation. God may not need our prayers but he has chosen to allow us to work in this way, as partners for good with him. Prayer is never wasted, though our prayers may not always be answered in the way that we would expect or like. Sometimes we pray for a long time and nothing seems to change. Maybe things seem to get worse. Yet God hears, receives and answers prayer in ways that we may never fully realise in this life. Even our imperfect or selfish prayers can be transformed and used, in God's mercy, because we are told that Jesus himself continually prays and intercedes for us.

Prayer is simply speaking directly to God, and telling him whatever we want to. The language doesn't matter. Our prayers will change as we mature, and the Holy Spirit will help us in our praying. Prayer is a life-line, for our children and for ourselves.

Pregnancy

Most Christian parents of growing girls, if they are honest, have a hidden fear that despite a loving and stable home background and careful training, their daughter might get pregnant out of wedlock. Others may believe that because of these very factors it could never happen to them.

Sadly, it could. Teenage pregnancy happens in the most caring and committed of families in all walks of life. And it happens in Christian families.

You may think that if your teenage daughter came to you with the news that she was pregnant, you would be devastated. You would feel as though your world had caved in. You would see all your hopes and plans for her turned to dust. You would agonise and wonder where you went wrong. You might angrily blame God for allowing this to happen, and question his lordship or his love. You might feel that your family life, ministry, your Christian witness or even your faith, was in ruins.

You'd be wrong. After the initial shock, you will rally and take stock. You'll collect your battered emotions and begin to reach out to your daughter. You'll help and support her in the decisions she faces. You'll find inner strength you never knew you had, and through your own suffering you'll find your heart is softer towards a suffering world. And you will find that, despite the storms that do their best to buffet and destroy you, your feet are firmly and securely planted on the rock that is Jesus Christ.

Premarital sex

Premarital sex seems to be widely accepted as the norm among consenting young people today. Often it is difficult to explain to a young person the standpoint of reserving sex for a committed marital relationship. It is difficult for a parent to be convincing on this issue when the trends of society, the child's peer group, and his or her own hyperactive hormones are telling a different story.

A well-established parent/child relationship is the best help to communication here, as elsewhere. So is the input of other respected older Christians – teachers, youth leaders, young married couples. Mostly, though, you will have to leave your children to draw their own conclusions and make their way through the minefield of teenage relationships, pressures and decisions. Teenagers are often more mature and have far more common sense than we give them credit for.

Pornography

Different people may have different ideas of what pornography is. Satan has been successful in perverting and twisting the human sexual nature which is a beautiful gift from God. We must protect our youngsters in every way we can from those who peddle in perversion for their own gain.

However, we must be careful not to over-react when we encounter the normal adolescent interest in sex. The odd 'girlie' mag, or suggestive note found in a pocket or a school bag, does not mean that your child is going off the rails. Discuss it with the child if you can do it in a calm, non-confrontational way. If you can't, better say nothing. Pray for the protection of your child's mind and morals and allow God to speak to him.

Also, pay close attention to your own reading material and film and video viewing – are you as careful as you ought to be?

Puberty

Puberty happens at different ages in different people, but it does seem a fact that its onset begins earlier now than 30 or 40 years ago.

A girl may begin to menstruate as young as 9 or 10, and boys may begin to enter adolescence a year or two later. If your child is an early developer, he or she will need a little extra understanding and tolerance to see them through. Many young people would like to stay children a little longer, and are resentful and anxious about becoming adults. Puberty is not easy for either child or parents, and lots of love, patience and humour is needed to see everyone safely through.

qQ

Quarrels

See **Arguments**

Rebellion

A certain amount of teen rebellion is normal and even healthy. Developing young personalities have to find their own identity, test their limits and push parental boundaries. They are not going to be carbon copies of anyone, and need to find their own feet.

But real pain sets in when a child rebels in a way that's potentially destructive to him- or herself and to others. Nothing hurts a parent more than a child set on rejecting all the values and standards instilled over years of care and commitment. It's bewildering, hurtful and devastating.

Christian parents need to be wise before the event, minimising any potential teenage rebellion by building and maintaining a strong relationship right through childhood. We need to listen to our children, hear their views and understand that their interpretation of life and values may be different from ours. Most rebels and their parents emerge at the other end without too many scars, and many rebellious teenagers turn into strong adults.

Reconciliation

See also
Forgiveness

Never close the door on any of your children. Whatever heartache and disappointment they have caused, however much they've let you down, nothing – absolutely nothing – is worth losing that relationship for. Bitterness and un-

74

forgiveness will harm you as much as, or more than, it harms your child, and it will also harm your relationship with God and with others.

If you feel you can't forgive, remember that God has forgiven you so much more. Read the parable of the prodigal son and realise a little of the father heart of God, which is a model for us human parents.

Rejection

Nothing hurts as much or leaves such an awful scar. Adopted children in particular carry the heavy burden of knowing that they were once, for whatever reason, given away. However loving the family they've been raised in, the knowledge will hurt and may surface in feelings of insecurity, leading to resentment and rebellion in the teen years. Feelings of rejection can also kick in after family break-ups, divorce, bereavement, or as a result of disability or bullying.

Counselling can make a world of difference, and there are gentle therapies such as reactional analysis that can help to reaffirm a sense of self-worth. Lots of TLC and, particularly, lots of prayer are vitally important. It may take a lot of time, patience and understanding to bring a young person to the place where he or she feels fully accepted, valued and loved, no matter what has gone before. But it can be done.

Respect

We all like our growing children to respect us, as parents and as people, and it's right that they should. Maybe respect is caught rather than taught. A child will learn best to respect others if he sees that his parents respect people even if their lifestyles, beliefs and values differ from their own. A child needs to know that he or she is respected by both parents too.

Responsibility (sense of)

A child can learn responsibility for small things quite early on, e.g. taking care of their possessions or earning and saving pocket money for things they would like. The care of pets is a good way of learning to be responsible, though this may need a bit of firm parental guidance and overseeing.

Some youngsters become responsible earlier than others. There may be a few lapses along the way – don't forget they're not quite adult yet, and you can't put an old head on young shoulders.

Role model

Like it or not, the same-sex parent of a child will be its first role model. This is no light responsibility and should be faced with honesty and full commitment. Our children accept our attitudes and behaviour as the norm.

Let's make sure there are no double-standards in our lives. As adults and parents, we need role models too. We have the best role model of all time in Jesus Christ.

Rules

Rules are needed, though they won't always be kept, and there may be times when we have to accept that they may be bent, misunderstood or ignored. No system is perfect, but a fairly flexible system of family rules is worth working towards.

Remember, though, that rules are no substitute for a living, growing, changing, listening, communicating relationship with our children.

I recently read a quote which I thought was very wise. It simply said 'rules without relationship lead to rebellion'.

Runaways

There can't be a much worse nightmare for a parent than a missing child. It happened to us, and though in our case our immediate fears were fairly quickly laid to rest, a long period of painful readjustment was to follow. I can't imagine a worse agony than never to know what has happened to your child.

Fortunately, most runaways are traced fairly quickly and do return home unscathed. For those who wait, a strong support system and/or counselling can be a lifeline.

Most young people don't stop to think things through, and taking off might seem the answer to areas of conflict that have become unbearable. However, no one should let themselves be ruled by the constant fear that their child might do a runner. Christian parents have the great advantage of having access to a Father who is also a Father to their children, and can work wonders in the most impossible of situations.

Self-esteem

Self-esteem can be a fragile thing needing lots of reinforcement. There seem to be pitfalls and put-downs waiting at every turn.

Children need to feel loved and precious. They need to feel they are valued for themselves, not for what they might achieve or become, and however they behave. They need to know that they are OK as individuals and that they don't have to emulate anyone else. They need to be encouraged in their particular gifts and talents, not made to feel inadequate for what they can't do or aren't interested in. They need to be affirmed as unique persons made by God in his own image, and with a plan especially designed for them by God.

Sex

Your child will grow up in a world and society dominated and obsessed by sex. Sadly, it will not always be sex in the way that God ordained it, as a special and wonderful gift to be used and enjoyed by a husband and wife in a lifelong commitment. You can't protect your child from the evils of the world, and sooner or later, they will know something of homosexuality, perversion, and other ways in which Satan has twisted this gift.

It's dangerous to assume that a Christian home guarantees that a child does not fall into sexual sin. Sadly, in our fallen world this may not be the case.

However, a loving, stable, Scripture-based up-bringing is still the best safeguard we can give our children. And remember, when there are casualties, we also have a loving, forgiving God who can restore and make all things new.

Sex education

Sex education goes on throughout childhood, and it's not just about dutifully answering questions as they arise (though this is important too). Children need to know that you are comfortable and happy with your own sexuality and they need the security of knowing that their two parents are totally committed to one another in a permanent way. This is the best kind of sex education a child can have.

Sharing

However honest and close your relationship, your teenager is unlikely to share every single experience, problem, thought and opinion with you. Some things you'll hear about, but others they'll share with their peer group or even another adult. It's their prerogative, so don't pry and don't feel rejected. Be honest – did you share everything with your parents?

Sibling rivalry

Even the best of families have their share of sibling rivalry – unless you happen to have only one child. However fair, loving and committed we try to be, there'll be times when your children feel they are competing for your love/time/attention/approval. They may outgrow it, or there may always be an edge of competition between them. Try to minimise it by spending some time alone with each child, giving them your full attention and making them feel they are of paramount importance. Also beware of holding up one child as an example to another or boasting of a sibling's achievements/abilities/gifts/talents. Better maybe to praise your child directly rather than to their brothers and sisters.

Step-parents

With divorce on the increase, family structures (even in Christian families) can become increasingly complicated. Many families have a step-parent, and there may be step-siblings as well as half-brothers and sisters. The comings and goings of children between natural and step-parents can confuse the issue even further.

If you're a step-parent, don't try to be another parent to your stepchildren. They will have an equivalent parent of their own (or will have had, when there's been bereavement). In either case, you're likely to be resented if you try to fill the missing person's place in their lives.

The best you can aim for is to be a friend to them; there if they need you but not pushing it if they don't. Don't flaunt your relationship with the parent – you don't have to prove anything. Try to understand any guilt your spouse may feel, and be prepared to take a back seat now and then if the children need extra attention. Above all, don't feel guilty if you can't feel

Sibling Rivalry

the same towards your stepchildren as you do to your natural ones. The relationship is not the same. Step-families can be hard work, but sticking to it can pay dividends and be very rewarding, given time.

Support

Independent as teenagers like to think they are, parental support is crucial. It's easy to support a child when they are going the way you want, and you approve of what they're doing. But they will need support even more when they make mistakes and take a wrong turn in life. The right support, rather than criticism or condemnation, will get them back on track again, although it might not be the track you'd hoped for.

Parents sometimes need support too, when things get tough. Don't be too proud to ask for help from family and friends or from professionals. Especially, learn to lean hard on the support that God offers to all those who will trust in him.

t T

Taking for granted

Most teenagers notoriously take for granted everything they have, including the love and care of their families. It's tough to take sometimes, but appreciation will come with maturity.

There's another kind of taking for granted that we as parents are sometimes guilty of. We can take it for granted that our child's views, beliefs and ambitions will be the same as ours, and when it doesn't happen we can be confused and dismayed. Again, we need to listen to our child and realise that he or she is an individual.

Temperament

Years ago I read a book on temperament which has been an enormous help in understanding people, especially those I have difficulty with. Knowing and recognising the four different basic temperaments (though we're all mixtures) is helpful in realising that some of our attitudes and behaviour are down to differences in temperament rather than being right or wrong. Our children's temperaments can differ from ours, and their strengths and weaknesses will differ from ours too. The presence of the Holy Spirit in the life of an individual will balance out the problem areas in the different temperaments, and counteract our human weaknesses with God's strength.

Spirit Controlled Temperament and *Spirit Controlled Family* both by Tim La Haye.

Tensions

See also **Sibling rivalry, Step-families**

Where there are teenagers there'll be tensions. At times we're all frustrated and feeling we're not coping in the right way and just muddling along. Maybe we need to lean harder on God, handing over to him the things we feel we can't manage ourselves.

Try mentally wrapping your tensions and frustrations into a big bundle, taking it to the foot of the Cross and laying it down there. It's tempting to pick it up and try to carry it again, so we may need to repeat this over and over.

There can also be tension areas between teenage siblings, or teens and younger brothers and sisters. While we do have to keep an eye out for the younger ones, it's sometimes best not to be in too much of a hurry to intervene. Sometimes they're better sorting things out for themselves.

Times

In family life, there's a time to discipline and a time to forgive. There's a time to correct and a time to affirm. A time to work and a time to relax and rest. A time to speak and a time to be quiet. There's a time to weep, and a time to laugh with a child – not at them. There's a time to hold on and a time to let go.

Only God can give us the wisdom we need to discern the times. Read Ecclesiastes 3.

Travel

Most teenagers want to see the world (though this is another thing we mustn't take for granted). It's good to start in a well-supervised

84

way, with school trips, exchange visits, field trips and so on. Mission projects and volunteer work are also an excellent way of launching out, and there'll be plenty of support.

Sooner or later, it's on the cards that your child will want to travel more independently. It's a gut-wrenching time for parents, saying goodbye to someone off on their travels with not much more than a backpack, a few contact addresses, and hopes of high adventure. Travel in a group is safest. Some friendly contacts at the place of destination make a great jumping-off point, and are a comfort to parents. A young traveller needs to be clued up and know who to get in touch with in case of accident, illness or emergency. Most of them come to no harm, return safely and have a whale of a time.

Trust

The vexed question of trust can develop into a vicious circle. Teenagers want to be trusted with more freedom and a greater measure of taking responsibility for themselves, and kick against restrictions while protesting their trustworthiness. A parent wishes to see a little more evidence of the same before granting trust. Round and round it goes.

Perhaps it's best to begin by trusting a child in small ways first and building on that. Trust does have to be earned, but sometimes we can give them the benefit of the doubt. When trust has been broken it will be hard to regain it, but not impossible. You will both have learned something.

TV

We may think our teenagers spend far too much time on computer games or surfing the internet. Many of us parents would be rather shocked if we added up the hours a week we spend watching TV or videos. Teenagers have a sharp eye for hypocrisy and won't be slow to point it out.

u U

Unconditional love

Maybe the parent/child relationship is the best illustration we have, humanly speaking, of unconditional love. Even so, it's just a pale reflection of the love offered to us by our Father God.

God's love has no conditions whatsoever. It is poured out alike on every person ever born, whatever our colour, race or creed and however we look, think or behave. The only limit to God's love is our capacity and willingness to accept and receive it. Most of us humans are so screwed up that we cannot believe that anyone could love us in this way. We can only convince others of this love by first receiving it for ourselves and then passing it on to the people we're in contact with. This is beyond us in our own strength, but perfectly possible with the help of God's spirit. We need to know we're loved before we can love in return. We love God because he first loved us. Our children will learn to love when they are themselves loved, by us as parents and beyond us, by God.

Understanding

We all long to be truly known and understood. A lot of harm can result from misunderstandings, and it's not always easy to explain or even to understand ourselves. Teenage children are especially vulnerable and in need of understanding. They're also likely to be unfairly judged – and sometimes resent very much the labels that tend to be stuck to them – ungrateful, lazy, selfish, thoughtless, etc. Let's try to remember how it felt to be teenagers ourselves. Let's concentrate on the positive things, listen to them, affirm the people they are and look forward to the people they're going to be.

University

See also **Empty Nest Syndrome, Leaving, Letting go**

A whole new ball game begins with your child's first term (or semester) at uni. You'll go through a time of real mourning for the end of an era. Talking to other parents helps. Mums sobbing on each other's shoulders over supermarket trolleys is not an uncommon sight in September or early October. You will probably have seen him or her off with a carload of clothes, duvets, TV, video recorder, CD-player, computer, pots and pans and food, not to mention the Dettox, dishcloths and scouring powder.

For now, you've done all you can. The next hurdle may be the tearful phone calls or pathetic little notes when homesickness kicks in. That, too, is fairly inevitable, and that, too, will pass. Be there to listen, maybe visit in a few weeks, but don't jump to the conclusion that your child has made a mistake and rush to bail them out.

They'll find their feet and so will you. Concentrate on your own life and your own interests, or take up something new. It won't be long until Christmas!

vV

Vegetarianism

See also **Diet**

Many young people today are opting for vegetarianism. (Some parents may be vegetarians too.) If your child makes this choice, respect it. It may not last or it may not work for them, but it has to be their decision. Many teenagers do feel strongly about the way livestock for meat is raised and treated.

Your child can get all the necessary protein without traditional meat and two veg. Cheese, eggs, milk, fish (if permitted) soya products and pulses will provide the balance they need.

Violence

Monitoring a child's exposure to violence on TV or video is wise. We also need to watch our own viewing – it's easy for our attitudes and reactions to harden if watching violence of any kind becomes commonplace.

If there's any suspicion that a child of any age is being bullied (even verbally), take action. A child persistently bullied may react by behaving in the same way to others. Sticking up for oneself is fine, but the child needs to know there's back-up.

wW

Waiting up

See also
Late nights

Most of us parents have done our share of waiting up, watching the clock and worrying as the minutes tick by when our son or daughter is not home by the appointed time. Most times our worries are needless – a detour had to be made to drop off someone else, a car gave trouble, a bus was missed. Most teenagers genuinely won't know what all the fuss was about – they knew they were all right, so why were you worrying? Don't you trust them or something?

A few rules need to be established and observed. You need to know where they're going, who they're with, and the approximate time of their return. If there's a deadline, they ought to respect it. If something unforeseen happens to cause delay, they should let you know.

In these days of the mobile phone, it's a simple solution for your child to take one along when he or she goes out, so that you can be in two-way contact.

Weight

See also **Diet**

Both boys and girls can be weight conscious in their teens. They may even become slightly obsessive about diet and about exercise and working out. This is OK, provided the food they eat contains the nutrients a rapidly growing person needs. Make sure that the food in

90

the house is healthy stuff – plenty of fresh fruit and veg, and properly balanced and cooked meals.

A word of warning – never tease or comment in a negative way about the size, weight or shape of a teenager. It's a sensitive area, and the most innocent of remarks can cause problems or even trigger off some kind of eating disorder – though usually there are more serious underlying problems to begin with. You do need to seek help if your child is losing weight, if he or she always insists on taking food to their room to eat, if he or she hides or conceals food or induces vomiting.

The Eating Disorder Association, First Floor, Wensum House, 103 Prince of Wales Road, Norwich, Norfolk NR1 1DW (01603) 621414

The Anorexia and Bulimia Nervosa Association, Tottenham Women and Health Centre Annexe, Tottenham, London N15 4RK

Youth Helpline: (01603) 765050 Monday – Friday, 4-6pm

Work

Some form of holiday, weekend or Saturday work is an excellent idea, augmenting income and requiring discipline to get out of bed and out of the house. It also gives a child a sense of independence and some idea of what it will eventually be like out there in the working world. They'll also gain valuable insights and ideas of what they are suited for, and what they feel they could or couldn't do as a future career.

Worry

See also **Anxiety**

I doubt any of us avoid it altogether as parents, however relaxed, confident, clued-up and laid-back we might be. But with God in our lives we have an antidote to worry.

God is more involved and concerned with our child's life than we are ourselves. He also understands perfectly and knows the end from the beginning. His thoughts are not our thoughts – fortunately!

It's the greatest privilege to be able to bring all our worries about our children to God in prayer. Let's try not to direct God, telling him what's best for our child and what we want done. He knows better than we do. Let God be God. Bringing our fears and worries to him, asking him to take the burden and work out the situation in whatever way he thinks best, is the very best prayer we can make for our children.

Worship

The way our teenagers and their friends like to worship God may not be our cup of tea at all! Their worship may be more free and uninhibited, more unconventional in its expression. It will almost certainly be louder!

Christian teenagers today often seem to be able to 'tune in' to God in a way not so easy to their more hidebound, tradition-based elders. There are possibly many lessons we can learn from observing and joining our young people in their chosen styles of worship.

X – The unknown quantity

See **Occult**

Youth groups

I am unashamedly in favour of Christian youth groups, whether a church-based or an independent organisation like Crusaders (which has as patrons Cliff Richard and Steve Chalke). A Christian teenager who isn't in one is missing out on lots. Youth groups can provide friendship, fun, challenge, growth, opportunities, wise nonparental counsel and advice from leaders, and much more. There'll be activities, teaching, holidays, weekends, projects, houseparties and all kinds of exciting spin-offs. If you like young people and there isn't such a group locally, you could even consider starting one yourself.

zZ

Zits

Zits, or other kinds of acne or skin eruption, loom large in the life of teenagers and cause more distress than they seem to merit. That little spot or blemish may seem almost invisible to you, but it's a disaster to someone off to a party, especially if there's someone there they really want to impress. Offering sympathy and a dab of cover make-up is better than laughing it off. Zits, like much else in the teenage years, are mostly down to hormones. They're annoying but temporary, and they, too, will pass.